SUZI ESZTERHAS

is a professional wildlife photographer, based in California and the UK.
She specialises in documenting the family lives of endangered species
and is well-known for her unprecedented work with newborn animals.
Her photographs are published in books, magazines and newspapers
all over the world. She has won numerous awards and is represented by
the world's leading natural history agencies. Suzi is on the road
for many months of the year, undertaking commissions
and leading instructional photography tours and workshops
everywhere from the poles to the tropics.
The EYE ON THE WILD series is her first project for Frances Lincoln.

To my mother, Gerri, for her endless love

JANETTA OTTER-BARRY BOOKS

Eye on the Wild: Brown Bear copyright © Frances Lincoln Limited 2012
Text and photographs copyright © Suzi Eszterhas 2012

The right of Suzi Eszterhas to be identified as the author and photographer of this work
has been asserted by her in accordance with the Copyright, Designs and Patents Act,
1988 (United Kingdom).]

First published in Great Britain and in the USA in 2012 by
Frances Lincoln Children's Books, 4 Torriano Mews,
Torriano Avenue, London NW5 2RZ
www.franceslincoln.com

This paperback edition first published in Great Britain in 2012

A catalogue record for this book is available from the British Library.

ISBN 978-1-84780-308-5

Set in Stempel Schneidler

Printed in China

1 3 5 7 9 8 6 4 2

BROWN BEAR

Suzi Eszterhas

F

FRANCES LINCOLN
CHILDREN'S BOOKS

Far away in the mountains of Alaska, in the middle of winter, two baby brown bears are born. It is so cold outside that they spend the first few months of their lives tucked away in a warm and cosy den, fast asleep next to Mum. They don't venture into the outside world until spring arrives, and the weather is getting warmer. When they do eventually leave their den, Mum stays close beside them.

The baby bears are called 'cubs' and look a lot like teddy bears. Even though they are five months old when they leave the den, they are still very small and need their mum's constant love and attention. They will stay right by her side for the next two years.

The cubs love their mum's milk so much that, when they are drinking, they hum to themselves contentedly. They are rather like happy cats purring. Mum will keep feeding them lots of milk until they are almost as big as she is.

Mum takes her babies everywhere she goes and they have many exciting adventures. They cross rivers, explore fields of flowers, laze around in grass meadows and even go to the beach to play in the sand. But Mum is always watching over them to make sure they stay safe and don't get into trouble.

While the family is out exploring, the two young bears eat a lot of fresh, green grass. The grass is crunchy and tastes deliciously sweet. It is a very healthy food and helps to wake up their tummies after their long, winter sleep.

The young cubs are bursting with energy. They love to play-fight, chase each other and climb about on logs. The games they play are great fun, but they also help the bears to grow big and strong and they teach them essential survival skills that will be important when they have to survive on their own.

After all their adventures, it's time for a nap. Mum guards her cubs while they are fast asleep – always on the look-out for danger. A brown bear mum is one of the bravest mums on Earth and she will do anything to protect her babies.

When autumn arrives, it's time to go fishing. Mum is an expert! When she spots a tasty-looking salmon in the river, she charges into the water at top speed and makes a huge splash. She uses her long claws as hooks to catch the fish when it tries to swim away.

A brown bear likes nothing more than a
tasty salmon to eat – and the two cubs love
the taste of it right away. So Mum is kept busy
catching enough fish to feed herself and her two
hungry offspring. The rich oil in the fish will
give the family the fat they need to stay warm
throughout the freezing, cold winter to come.

But brown bears don't eat only salmon. They eat lots of different foods. They even love to eat clams and, on warm summer days, Mum takes her youngsters to the beach to find these sweet treats. Looking for clams is like a treasure hunt and the cubs use their paws to turn over rocks and dig deep in the sand.

The cubs are growing bigger and braver every day and, after nearly two years, they are almost as big as Mum. But they are still young and have a great deal more to learn before she lets them out into the wide world on their own.

As the cubs grow older, Mum teaches them to fish for their own salmon and they spend day after day in the river. Fishing lessons aren't as much fun as playing, but the cubs need to learn how to find the best fishing spots and the different ways to catch their prey.

Catching fish is not easy! At first, the cubs splash about too much and scare the fish away. Or they jump and miss, so a lot of fish manage to escape. But eventually the cubs get really good at fishing – almost as good as Mum.

When the cubs are two-and-a-half years old, Mum's work is finally done. She has taught them how to fish, how to find clams and other food, how to make a winter den, and how to stay out of danger. Now Mum has to leave them. But the two cubs will stay together for a while longer.

The two young bears still like to play-fight just like when they were babies. They are careful not to hurt each other and use their huge paws like boxing gloves. This helps them to learn how to protect themselves now that Mum has gone.

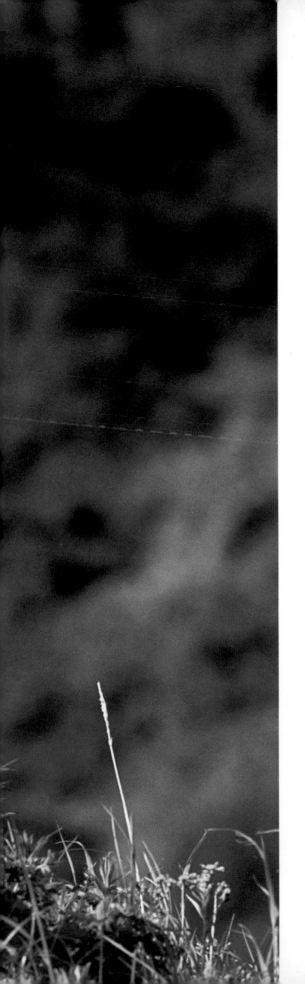

The young bears celebrate
their third birthday together,
hidden away in a warm winter
den, where they spend as long
as five months fast asleep.
At last, spring arrives and
it's warm enough to venture
outside. They leave the den
and say goodbye to each other.
Now they are ready for their
biggest adventure yet – starting
families of their own.

More about Brown Bears

- Brown bears live in North America, Europe and Asia.

- Brown bears are the second-largest bears in the world, after polar bears. Male brown bears can weigh over 455 kilograms or 1,000 pounds and stand nearly 3 metres or 10 feet tall.

- Brown bears are not always brown. Their thick fur may be black, cinnamon, auburn, or even blond.

- Brown bears will eat almost anything. Most of their diet is fish, berries, herbs, roots, nuts, flowers, grasses, and other vegetation. But they also eat insects, honey, small mammals and even elk.

- Brown bears have very good noses and can smell things from nearly 1.5 kilometres or a mile away.

- In early autumn, when brown bears are feeding on salmon, they can gain up to 1.4 kilograms or 30 pounds a day. They will live off this fat during their long winter hibernation.

- During hibernation, a bear's body functions slow down, and its heartbeat drops from 40–70 beats a minute to about 8–12 beats a minute.

- Brown bears are endangered because people are hunting them and destroying their home.

- For more information visit http://www.raincoast.org

Collect all the books in the EYE ON THE WILD series – a brilliant introduction to animals in the wild, from birth to adulthood

Cheetah
ISBN 978-1-84780-307-8

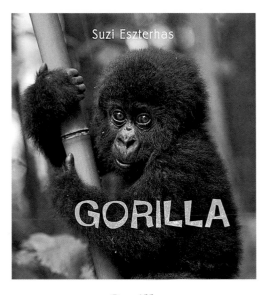

Gorilla
ISBN 978-1-84780-305-4

Brown Bear
ISBN 978-1-84780-308-5

Lion
ISBN 978-1-84780-311-5

Frances Lincoln titles are available from all good bookshops.
You can also buy books and find out more about your favourite titles,
authors and illustrators on our website: www.franceslincoln.com